Dedication

"I would like to dedicate this program to all those who ever struggled with learning a foreign language and to Wolfgang Karfunkel"

Also by Yatir Nitzany

Conversational Spanish Quick and Easy

Conversational French Quick and Easy

Conversational Italian Quick and Easy

Conversational German Quick and Easy

Conversational Russian Quick and Easy

Conversational Yiddish Quick and Easy

Conversational Hebrew Quick and Easy

Conversational Arabic Quick and Easy
Lebanese Dialect

Conversational Brazilian-Portuguese Quick and Easy

THE MOST ADVANCED, REVOLUTIONARY TECHNIQUE TO MASTER CONVERSATIONAL BRAZILIAN-PORTUGUESE

YATIR NITZANY

Copyright © 2012
Yatir Nitzany
All rights reserved.
ISBN-10: 149935200X
EAN-13: 978-1499352009

Printed in the United States of America

FORWARD

ABOUT MYSELF

For many years I struggled to learn Spanish, and still knew no more than about 20 words and consequently was extremely frustrated. One day I stumbled upon this method as I was playing around with word combinations. Suddenly I came to the realization that every language has a certain core group of words that are most commonly used in a language, and simply by learning them, one could gain ability to engage in fluent communication..

I discovered which those words were, narrowed them down to 350, and that once memorized, one could then connect and create one's own sentences. THE VARIATIONS WERE and ARE, INFINITE!!! By using this incredibly simple technique I could converse at a proficient level and speak Spanish. Within a week I astonished my Spanish speaking friends with my new found ability. The following semester I enrolled at my university for a Spanish Speaking Course. I applied the same principles I learned in that class (grammar, additional vocabulary, future and past tense, etc.) to the 350 words I already had memorized and by doing so, perfected my Spanish to a level far greater than I had ever hoped, I immediately felt as if I had grown wings and learned how to fly!!!!! At the end of the semester we took a class trip to San José, Costa Rica. I was like a fish in water, while the rest of my classmates were floundering and still struggling to converse. Throughout the following months I again applied the same principle to other languages, French, Portuguese, Italian, and Arabic all of which I now speak proficiently thanks to this very simple technique.

This method is by far the fastest way to master fluent conversation. There is no other technique that compares to my concept. It is effective, it worked for me and it will work for you. Be consistent with my program and you too will succeed the way I and many, many others have.

Contents

Introduction to the Program 8

Introduction to the Portuguese Language 11

Memorization Made Easy 13

Note to the Reader 15

The Program 16

Building Bridges 38

Basic Grammatical Requirements of the
Portuguese Language. 42

Reading and Pronunciation in Portuguese 47

Now you are on your own 51

Conclusion 53

INTRODUCTION TO THE PROGRAM

People often dream about learning a foreign language, but never do. Whatever the reason is, it's time to set it aside and with my new method, you will have enough time and you will not fail. You will actually learn how to speak the fundamentals of the language, and speak the language fluently in as little as a few days. Of course you won't speak perfect Portuguese at first, but you will certainly gain significant proficiency. For example, if you travel to Brazil or Portugal, you will almost effortlessly be able engage in basic 'fluent' communication with the locals, and you will no longer be intimidated with culture shock. It's time to relax. Learning a language is a valuable skill and a form of communication that connects people of multiple cultures around the world.

How does my method work? Well, I have taken twenty-seven of the most used languages and distilled out of them the 350 most commonly used words in any language. This whole process took three years of observation and research, and during that time I have determined which words I felt were most important for this method of basic 'fluent' communication. In that time, I chose these words in such a way that they are structurally interrelated, and when combined, they form sentences. Thus once you succeed in memorizing them, then you will be able to combine these words and form your own sentences. The words are spread over 20 pages. In fact, there are just nine basic words that will effectively build bridges, enabling you to speak in an understandable manner (please see Building Bridges on

Introduction to the Program

page #38). The words will also correspond easily in sentences, for example, enabling you to ask simple questions, etc. I have also created *Memorization Made Easy* techniques for this program in order to assist with the memorization of the vocabulary (Page #13). **Please also see page #47, in order to gain proficiency in the reading and pronounciation, of the Portuguese language,** prior to starting this program.

My book is mainly intended for basic 'present tense' vocal communication, meaning anyone can easily use it to 'get by' linguistically while visiting a foreign country, without learning the entire language. You will be 100 percent understandable to native speakers, which is your aim. One disclaimer: this is NOT a grammar book, though it does address minute and essential grammar rules (Please see Basic Grammatical Requirements of the Portuguese Language on page #42). Therefore, understanding complex sentences with obscure words in a language is outside the scope of this book.

People who have tried this method have been successful, and by the time you finish this book, you will be 90 percent fluent and understandable in the Portuguese Language. This is the best basis to learn, not only the Portuguese language but any language. THIS IS AN ENTIRELY REVOLUTIONARY NO-FAIL CONCEPT, and your ability to place all the pieces of the puzzle together, will come with GREAT ease, especially if you use this program prior to beginning a Portuguese class.

THE PORTUGUESE LANGUAGE

Portuguese has over 200 million native speakers, as it is the sixth most common language in the world. The language originated from Latin roots, and became popular after a Roman invasion of the western region of the Iberian Peninsula (area known today as Portugal) during the 3rd century BC. The incoming Romans blended their language with that of the natives, so Portuguese began to modify. Traders of the time began to use the language, so it spread rapidly, making its way into Africa and Asia and eventually Brazil. In fact, before the language was officially modernized, it was more unique. Today, there are more traces of Greek and Latin and fewer words from the actual Portuguese language.

Spoken in: Portugal, Brazil, Angola, Mozambique, Guinea-Bissau, Cape Verde, and São Tomé and Príncipe

MEMORIZATION MADE EASY

There is no doubt the 350 words in my program are the required essentials in order to engage in fluent basic conversation in any foreign language. However, some people may experience difficulty in the memorization, and for this reason I created "Memorization Made Easy," this memorization technique will make this program so simple and fun that it's unbelievable! I have spread the words over the following 20 pages. Each page contains a vocabulary table of 10-15 words. Below every vocabulary box, sentences are composed from the words, on the page, that you had just studied. This aids greatly in the memorization. Once you succeed in memorizing the first page, then proceed to the second, upon completion of the second page, go back to the first and review, then proceed to the third page, after memorizing the third go back to the first and second and repeat, and so on.... As you continue along, begin to combine words and create your own sentences in your head. Every time you proceed to the following page, you will notice words from the previous pages will be present in those simple sentences as well, as repetition is one of the most crucial aspects in learning any foreign language. Upon completion of the following twenty pages, CONGRATULATIONS!!! you have absorbed the required words and gained fluent proficiency, **and are now able to create your 'own'** sentences and be able to say anything you wish in the Portuguese Language. THIS IS A CRASH COURSE IN CONVERSATIONAL PORTUGUESE, AND IT WORKS!

NOTE TO THE READER

The purpose of this book is merely to enable you to communicate in Portuguese. In the program itself (pages 16-40) you may notice that the composition of some of those sentences might sound rather clumsy. Please disregard it, this is intentional. These sentences were formulated in a specific way to serve two purposes; to facilitate in the easy memorization of the vocabulary AND to teach you how to combine the words in order to form your own sentences for fluent communication, rather than making complete literal sense in the English language.

The sole purpose of this program is for conversational use ONLY, and is based on the method of the mirror translation technique. These sentences, as well as the translations are NOT incorrect, just a little clumsy. Latin languages, Semitic languages, Anglo-Germanic languages, as well as a few others are compatible with the mirror translation technique.

This method surpasses any other known language learning technique that is currently out there on the market. Just stick with the program and you will achieve wonders!!!!!

THE PROGRAM

Lets Begin! "Vocabulary"
(memorize the vocabulary)

I	Eu
With you	Contigo
With him / wih her	Com Ele / Com Ela
With us	Com nós
For you	Para você
Without him	Sem ele
Without them	(Masc)Sem Eles / (Fem)Sem elas
Always	Sempre
Was	Estive
This	Isto
Is	Está / É
Sometimes	Algumas Vezes
Maybe	Talvez
Are you	Você está / Voce é
Better	Melhor
I am	Eu sou / Estou
He / She , her	Ele / Ela
From	De / Do

Sentences from the vocabulary (now you can speak the sentences and connect the words)

I am with you
Estou contigo

Sometimes I am with him
Algumas vezes estou com ele

Are you without them today?
Você está sem eles hoje?

Sometimes you are with us at the mall
Algumas vezes você está conosco o mall

This is for you
Isto e para você

I am always with her
Estou sempre com ela

I am from Manaus
Eu sou do Manaus

Are you from Brazil?
Você é do Brasil?

*Concerning eu sou,estou / é,esta & você está,voce é please refer to the permanent and temporary section on page #43.
*Please also see page #47, in order to gain proficiency in the reading and pronounciation, of the Portuguese language.

Conversational Portuguese Quick and Easy

I was	Estive
To be	Estar / Ser
The	O / A / Os / As
Same	Mesmo / Igual
Good	(M)Bom / (F)boa
Here	Aqui
It's	Está / É
And	E
Between	Entre
Now	Agora
Later / After	Depois
If	Se
Yes	Sim
Then	Então
Tomorrow	Amanhã
You	Você / Tu
Also / too / as well	Também

Between now and later
Entre agora e depois
If it's later, then it's better tomorrow
Se está tarde, então é melhor amanhã
This is good as well
Isto é bom também
To be the same
Estar igual
Yes, you are very good
Sim, você e muito bom
I was here with them
Eu estive aqui com eles
You and I
Você e eu
The same day
O mesmo dia

*Concerning *o, as, os & as* please refer to the *singular and plural* section on page #42.
*Concerning *estar, ser* please refer to the *permanent and temporary* section on page #43.

17

The Program

Me	Me / mim
Ok	Ok
Even if	Inclusive
Afterwards	Depois
Worse	Pior
Where	Onde
Everything	Tudo
Somewhere	Algum lugar
What	Que
Almost	Quase
There	Lá / Ali

Afterwards is worse
Depois é pior
Even if I go now
Inclusive eu vou agora
Where is everything?
Onde está tudo?
Maybe somewhere
Talvez em algum lugar
What? I am almost there
Que? Estou quase lá
Where are you?
Onde está você?

Conversational Portuguese Quick and Easy

House / Home	Casa
In	Em / Dentro
Car	Auto / Carro
Already	Já
Good morning	Bom dia
How are you?	Como está você?
Where are you from?	De onde é você
Today	Hoje
Hello	Alô / Olá / Oi
What is your name?	Qual é o seu nome?
How old are you?	Quantos anos você tem?
Son	Filho
Daughter	Filha
At	Em / (M)No / (F)Na
Very	Muito
Hard	Difícil / Duro
Without us	Sem nós

She is without a car, so maybe she is still at the house?
Ela está sem um carro, talvez ela está ainda em casa
I am in the car already with your son and daughter
Eu já estou no carro com teu filho e filha
Good morning, how are you today?
Bom dia, como está você hoje?
Hello, what is your name?
Oi, qual é seu nome?
How old are you?
Quantos anos você tem?
This is very hard, but it's not impossible
Isto é muito difícil, mas não é impossível
Where are you from?
De onde é você ?

*In Portuguese, in regards to the pronoun *your*, there are two ways of saying it; *tua*, or *seu* (**male**) *sua* (**female**). *Tua* is the informal *your*, use it when speaking to a friend or someone whom you know well. While *seu* and *sua* are the formal *your*, use it when speaking to an authority, professor, someone whom you just met, to someone you show respect.

*In Portuguese, *"it's not"* is flipped around *não é*, or *não esta*

The Program

Thank you	(M)Obrigado / (F)Obrigada
For / In order to	Para
Anything	Qualquer coisa / Tudo
It's	é / Isto é
Time	Tempo
But	Mas
No / Not	Não
I am not	Eu não estou / Eu não sou
Away	Longe / Distante
That	(M) Este, (F) Esta
Similar	Similar / Parecido
Other / Another	Outro / Um outro
Side	Lado
Until	Até
Yesterday	Ontem
Still	Ainda / Todavia
Since	Desde
Day	Dia
Before	Antes

Thanks for anything
Obrigado por tudo
It's almost time
É quase tempo
I am not here, I am away.
Eu não estou aqui, estou longe.
That is a similar house
Esta é uma casa parecida
I am from the other side
Estou do outro lado
But I was here until late yesterday
Mas eu estive aqui até tarde de noite de ontem
Since the other day
Desde o outro dia

I say / I am saying	Eu digo / Estou dizendo
What time is it?	Que horas são?
I want	Quero
Without you	Sem você
Everywhere	Em todo Lugar
I go / I am going	Eu vou / Estou indo
With	Com
My	(S)(M/F)Meu/Minha (P)(M/F)Meus/Minhas
Cousin	Primo
I need	Preciso
Right now	Neste momento
Night	Noite
To see	Ver
Light	Luz
Outside	Fora
That is	Isto é
Any	Qualquer
I see / I am seeing	Eu vejo / Estou vendo

I am saying no / I say no
Estou dizendo não / Eu digo não
I want to see this during the day
Eu quero ver isto durante o dia
I see this everywhere
Eu vejo isso em todos os lugares
I am happy without my cousins here
Estou feliz sem os meus primos aqui
I need to be there at night
Preciso estar lá à noite
I see light outside
Eu vejo luz lá fora
What time is it right now?
Que horas são agora?

*In Portuguese, placing the pronoun *I,eu* preceding a conjugated verb isn't required. For example *I want to use this*, will be *quero usar isto*, instead of *eu quero usar isto*. Although saying **eu** *quero usar* isn't incorrect. The same rule also applies for the pronouns; *you, he, she, them, we*. Read page #44 to learn more.

The Program

Place	Lugar
Easy	Fácil
To find	Encontrar
To look for/ To search	Procurar /Buscar
Near	Perto
To wait	Esperar
To sell	Vender
To use	Usar
To know	Saber
To decide	Decidir
Between	Entre
Both	Ambos / los dos
To	De

This place is easy to find
Este lugar e muito fácil de encotrar
I need to look for you next to the car
Eu preciso procurar por você próximo do carro
I am saying to wait until tomorrow
Eu estou dizendo para esperar até amanhã
It's easy to sell this table
É fácil vender esta mesa
I want to use this
Eu quero usar isto
I need to know where is the house
Eu preciso saber onde está a casa
I need to decide between the two places
Eu preciso decidir entre os dois lugares
I am very happy to know that everything is ok
Estou muito feliz em saber que tudo está bem

That/which* can also be used as relative pronouns, the translation in Portuguese is *que*. *I am very happy to know that everything is ok, estou muito feliz em saber **que tudo está bem.*

*In English, an infinitive verb is always preceded by *to; to want, to wait, to decide*. But in Portuguese and Spanish the *ar,er,ir* at the end of the verb makes it infinitive; *querer, esperar, decidir*. Occasionally you can place a *para* preceding the infinitive verb; *to wait, para esperar.*

Because	Porque
To buy	Comprar
Like this	Asi
**Them	They**	(M) Eles / (F) Elas
I can / Can I	Eu Posso / Posso?
Book	Livro
Mine	Meu
To understand	Entender / Compreender
Problem / Problems	Problema / Problemas
I do / I am doing	Eu faço / Eu estou fazendo
Of	(S)(M/F)Do/Da (P)(M/F)Dos,Das (N)De
To look	Olhar
Myself	Eu mesmo
Enough	Bastante
Food	Comida
Water	Agua
Hotel	Hotel

I like this hotel because I want to look at the beach
Eu gosto deste hotel porque eu quero olhar a praia
I want to buy a bottle of water
Eu quero comprar uma garrafa de água
Both of them have enough food
Ambos deles tem bastante comida
That is the book, and that book is mine
Isto é um livro, e este livro é meu
I need to understand the problem
Eu preciso entender o problema
I see the view of the city from the hotel
Eu vejo a vista da cidade do hotel
I can work today
Eu posso trabalhar hoje
I do my homework
Eu faço meu dever de casa

*In the Portuguese language certain words connect forming one. For example *of(de)+them(eles)=deles, of(de)+this(este)=deste*. To learn more about these connection, please refer to page #45.
*To learn more about the conjugation of *of* please refer to pages #42 & #45 to learn more

The Program

I like	Eu gosto
There is / There are	Há / Aqui está / Aqui estão / São
Family / Parents	Família / Pais
Why	Porque
To say	Dizer
Something	Algo / Alguma coisa
To go	Ir
Ready	Pronto
Soon / quickly	Rápido / Logo
To work	Trabalhar
Who	Quien
To know	Saber

I like to be at my house with my parents
Eu gosto de estar na minha casa com meus pais
I want to know why I need to say something important
Quero saber porque eu precesio dizer alguma coisa importante
I am there with him
Eu estou ali com ele
I am busy, but I need to be ready soon
Eu ocupado, mas preciso estar pronto rápido
I like to work
Gosto de trabalhar
Who is there?
Quem está lá?
I want to know if they are here, because I want to go outside
Eu quero saber se eles estão aqui, porque eu quero ir para fora
There are seven dolls
São sete bonecas

How much	Quanto
To bring	Trazer
With me	Comigo
Instead	Em vez
Only	Somente
When	Quando
Lunch	Almoço
Or	Ou
Were	Erão
Without me	Sem eu
Fast / Quickly	Rápido
Slow / Slowly	Devagar
Cold	Frio
Inside	Dentro
To eat	Comer
Hot	Quente
To Drive	Dirigir

How much money do I need to bring with me?
Quanto dinheiro eu preciso trazer comigo?
Instead of this cake, I like that cake
Em vez deste bolo, eu gosto daquile bolo
Only when you can
Somente quando pode
They were without me yesterday
Eles estavam sem mim ontem
I need to drive the car very fast or very slowly
Eu preciso dirigir o carro muito rápido ou muito devagar
It is cold inside the library
Está frio dentro da biblioteca
Yes, I like to eat this hot for my lunch
Sim, eu gosto comer isto quente para meu almoço

The Program

To answer	Responder
To fly	Voar
Like (*preposition*)	Como
To travel	Viajar
To learn	Aprender
How	Como
To swim	Nadar
To practice	Practicar
To play	Jogar
To leave	Deixar
Many / A lot	Muito / Muitas
I go to	Eu vou para
First	Primeiro
Time / Times	Vez / Vezes

I need to answer many questions
Eu preciso responder muitas preguntas
I want to fly today
Eu quero voar hoje
I need to learn how to swim at the pool
Eu preciso aprender como nadar na piscina
I want to learn everything about how to play better tennis
Eu quero aprender tudo sobre como jogar o melhor tennis
I want to leave this here for you when I go to travel the world
Eu quero deixar isto para você aqui quando eu vou viajar pelo mundo
Since the first time
Desde a primeira vez
The children are yours
As crianças são tuas

*ial*Pelo mundo* literally means *throughout the world*.

Nobody / Anyone	Ninguém
Against	Contra
Us	Nós
To visit	Visitar
Mom / Mother	Mamãe / Mãe
To give	Dar
Which	Qual
To meet	Conhecer
Someone	Alguém
Just	Apenas
To walk	Caminhar/ Andar
Around	Ao redor
Towards	Para
Than	Que
Nothing / Anything	Nada

Something is better than nothing
Algo é melhor que nada
I am against him
Eu estou contra ele
We go to visit my family each week
Vamos visitar minha familia cada semana
I need to give you something
Eu preciso te dar algo
Do you want to meet someone?
Você quer conhecer alguém?
I am here on Wednesdays as well
Eu estou aqui às quartas-feiras também
You do this everyday?
Você faz isso todos os dias?
You need to walk around, but not towards the house
Você precisa caminhar ao redor, mas não para a casa

Te - is a direct and indirect object pronoun, the person who is actually affected by the action which is being carried out. But the *te* comes before the verb. For example: *I love you, eu te amo.* Or *to give you, te dar.*

The Program

I have / I must	Eu tenho / Eu devo
Don't / Doesn't	Não
Friend	Amigo
To borrow	Emprestar
To look like	Parecer
Grandfather	Avô
To want	Querer
To stay	Ficar
To continue	Continuar
Way	Maneira/ Caminho
That's why	Por isso
To show	Mostrar
To prepare	Preperar
I am not going	Eu não vou

Do you want to look like Arnold?
Você quer parecer como Arnold?
I want to borrow this book for my grandfather
Eu quero emprestar este livro do meu avô
I want to drive and to continue on this way to my house
Eu quero dirigir para continuar neste caminho para minha casa
I have a friend, that's why I want to stay in São Paulo
Eu tenho um amigo, por isso eu quero estar aqui em São Paulo
I am not going to see anyone here
Eu não vou ver ninguém aqui
I need to show you how to prepare breakfast
Eu preciso te mostrar como preparar o café da manhã
Why don't you have the book?
Por que você não tem o livro?
That is incorrect, I don't need the car today
Isso é incorreto, eu não preciso do carro hoje

To remember	Lembrar
Your	(S)(MF)Teu/Tua (P)(M,F)Tues/Tuas
Number	Número
Hour	Hora
Dark / darkness	Escuro / Escuridão
About	Sobre
Grandmother	Avó
Five	Cinco
Minute / Minutes	Minuto / Minutos
More	Mais
To think	Pensar
To do	Fazer
To come	Vir
To hear	Escutar
Last	(M)Último /(F)Última

You need to remember your number
Você precisa lembrar teu número
This is the last hour of darkness
Esta é a última hora da escuridão
I want to come and to hear my grandmother speak Portuguese today
Eu quero vir para escutar a minha avó fala português
I need to think more about this, and what to do
Eu preciso pensar mais sobre isto, e o que fazer
From here until there, it's just five minutes
Daqui até ali, é apenas cinco minutos

The Program

To leave	Sair
Again	Outra vez / de novo
Brazil	Brasil
To take	Tomar
To try	Tentar
To rent	Alugar
Without her	Sem ela
We are	Estamos / Somos
To turn off	Apagar
To ask	Pedir
To stop	Parar
Permission	Permissão

He needs to go to rent a house at the beach
Ele precisa ir e alugar uma casa na praia
I want to take the test without her
Eu quero tomar um teste sem ela
We are here a long time
Nós estamos aqui por muito tempo
I need to turn off the lights early
Eu preciso desligar as luzes cedo
We want to stop here
Nós queremos parar aqui
We are from Brazil
Nós somos do Brasil
The same building
O mesmo edifício
I want to ask permission in order to leave
Quero pedir permissão para sair

To open	Abrir
To buy	Comprar
To pay	Pagar
To clean	Limpar
Without	Sem
Sister	Irmã
To hope	Esperar
To live	Viver
Nice to meet you	Prazer em conhecer lo
Name	Nome
Last name	Sobrenome
To return	Regressar
Enough	Suficiente
Door	Porta
Our	Nosso / Nossa
On	Em, sobre

I need to open the door for my sister
Eu preciso abrir a porta para minha irmã
I need to buy something
Eu preciso comprar alguma coisa
I want to meet your sisters
Eu quero conhecer tuas irmãs
Nice to meet you, what is your name and your last name?
Prazer em conhecer lo, qual é o seu nome e, o seu sobrenome?
To hope for the better in the future
Esperar para o melhor no futuro
I want to return from the United States and to live without problems in Brazil
Eu quero regressar dos Estados Unidos e viver sem problemas no Brasil
Why are you sad right now?
Porque voce està triste em neste momento?
Our house is on the mountain
Nossa casa é na montanha

*In Portuguese *on* is *em*, however *on the* is *no/na*. To learn more see page #45.

The Program

To happen	Ocorrer / acontecer
To order	Ordenar
To drink	Beber
Excuse me	Desculpa
Child	Criança
Woman	Mulher
To begin / To start	Começar
To finish	Terminar
To help	Ajudar
To smoke	Fumar
To love	Amar
To talk / To Speak	Falar

This needs to happen today
Isto precisa acontecer hoje
Excuse me, my child is here as well
Desculpe, minha criança está aqui também
I need to begin soon and to be able to finish at three o'clock in the afternoon
Eu preciso começar rápido e poder para acabar às três horas da tarde
I want to learn how to speak Portuguese
Eu quero apprender como falar Português
I don't want to smoke again
Eu não quero fumar outra vez
I want to help
Eu quero ajudar
I love you
Eu te amo
I see you
Eu te vejo
I need you
Eu preciso de ti

*In Portuguese; child is *criança*, son is *filho* and *daughter* is *filha*.

To read	Ler
To write	Escrever
To teach	Ensinar
To close	Fechar
To turn on	Acender / Ligar
To prefer / To choose	Preferir
To put	Por / colocar
Less	Menos
Sun	Sol
Month	Mês
I talk / I speak	Eu Falo
Exact	(M)Exato / (F)exata

I need this book to learn how to read and write in Portuguese because I want to teach in Brazil
Eu preciso deste livro para ler e escrever em português porque eu quero ensinar no Brasil

I want to close the door of the house and not to turn on the light
Eu quero fechar a porta da casa e nao apagar as luzes

I prefer to put the gift here
Eu prefiro por o presente aqui

I want to pay less than you for the dinner
Eu quero pagar menos que você para o jantar

I speak with the boy and the girl in Spanish
Eu falo com o menino e a menina em espanhol

There is sun outside today
Há sol lá fora hoje

Is it possible to know the exact date
É possível saber a data exata

*In English adjectives usually preceed the verb, in Portuguese it's usually the opposite. Exact date, data exata / Blue car, carro azul.

The Program

To exchange	Trocar / Cambiar
To call	Chamar
Brother	Irmão
Dad	Papai
To sit	Sentar
Together	Juntos
To change	Trocar
Of course	Claro
Welcome	Bemvindo
During	Durante
Years	Anos
Sky	Céu
Up	Encima
Down	Abaixo
Sorry	Desculpe
To follow	Seguir
Him / Her	Lo /La
Big	Grande
New	Novo
Never	Jamais / Nunca

I never want to exchange this money at the bank
Eu nunca quero trocar este dinheiro no banco
I want to call my brother and my dad today
Eu quero chamar meu irmão e meu papai hoje
Of course I can come to the theater, and I want to sit together with you and your sister
Claro eu posso vir a teatro, e eu quero sentar junto contigo e com tua irmã
I need to look below in order to see your new house
Eu preciso olhar em abaixo para ver tua casa nova
I can see the sky from the window
Eu posso ver o céu da janela
I am sorry, but he wants to follow her to the store
Desculpe, mas ele quer segui-la até a loja

*In Portuguese, *lo* and *la* are used as direct masculine, feminine, and neuter object pronouns. Meaning; *him, her,* or *it*. To see him, *vê-lo* / to follow her, *segui-la* / to hold it, *mantê-lo*. The *r* at the end of the infinitive verb is removed.

To allow	Permitir / deixar
To believe	Crer
Morning	Manhã
Except	Exceto
To promise	Prometer
Good night	Boa noite
To recognize	Reconhecer
People	Pessoas
To move	Mover / Mudar
Far	Distante
Different	Diferente
Man	Home
To enter	Entrar
To receive	Receber
Throughout	Em todo
Good afternoon	Boa tarde
Through	Atravez
Free	Gratis

I need to allow him to go with us, he is a different man now
Eu preciso deixar ele ir conosco, ele é um homem diferente
I believe everything except for this
Eu preciso acreditar em tudo exceto para isto
I must promise to say good night to my parents each night
Eu preciso prometer de dizer boa noite a meu pais cada noite.
They need to recognize the people from Brazil very quickly
Eles precisam que recohnecer as pessoas do Brasil muito rapidamente
I need to move your cat to a different chair
Eu preciso mudar seu gato para uma cadeira diferente
They want to enter the competition and receive a free book
Eles querem entrar na competiçao e receber um livro gratis
I see the sun throughout the morning from the kitchen
Eu vejo o sol em toda manhã pelo cozinha
I go into the house but not through the yard
Eu vou por dentro da casa mas não através o jardim

The Program

To wish	Desejar
Bad	Mal / mau
To Get	Conseguir
To forget	Esquecer
Everybody	Todos
Although	Embora
To feel	Sentir
Great	Grande
Next	Próximo
To like	Gostar
In front	Em frente
Person	Pessoa
Behind	Atras
Well	Bem
See you soon / Goodbye	Vejo você logo/Tchau
Restaurant	Restaurante
Bathroom	Banheiro

I don't want to wish you anything bad
Eu não quero desejar a você nada de mal
I must forget everybody from my past so I can feel well
Devo esquecer todo mundo do meu pasado para me sentir bem
I am next to the person behind you
Eu estou próximo da pessoa atrás de você
There is a great person in front of me
Aqui esta uma grande pessoa na minha frente
I say goodbye to my friends
Eu digo adeus aos meus amigos
In which part of the restaurant is the bathroom?
Em que parte do restuarante esta o banheiro?
She has to get a car before the next year
Ela tem que conseguir um carro antes do próximo ano
I want to like the house, but it is very small
Eu quero gostar desta casa, mas esta muito pequeno

Conversational Portuguese Quick and Easy

To remove	Remover / Retirar
Please	Por favor
Beautiful	(M)Lindo/(F)Linda
To lift	Levantar
Include / Including	Incluir /Incluindo
Belong	Pertencer
To hold	Segurar
To check	Revisar
Small	Pequeno
Real	Real / Verdade
Week	Semana
Size	Tamanho
Even though	Mesmo que
Doesn't	Não
So	Então
Price	Preço

She wants to remove this door please
Por favor, ela quer remover esta porta
This doesn't belong here, I need to check again
Isto não pertencer aqui, preciso revisar outra vez
This week the weather was very beautiful
Esta semana, o tempo estava muito bonito
I need to know which is the real diamond
Eu preciso saber qual é o verdadeiro diamante
We need to check the size of the house
Eu preciso revisar o tamanho desta casa
I want to lift this, so you must hold it high
Eu quero levantar isto, por isso você deve para mantê-lo alto
I can pay this although the price is expensive
Eu posso pagar isto, embora o preço e caro
Including everything, is this price correct?
Incluindo tudo, este é preço está correto

BUILDING BRIDGES

In building bridges, we take these six conjugated verbs, which have been selected after studies I have conducted for several months in order to determine which verbs are most commonly conjugated, and which are then automatically followed by an infinitive verb. For example once you know how to say, *I Need, I Want, I Can, I Like,* it will enable you to connect words and say almost anything you want more proper and understandable. The following three pages contain these 6 conjugated verbs in first, second, third, fourth, and fifth person, as well as some sample sentences. Please complete the program prior to venturing onto this section.

I want	Quero
I need	Preciso
I can	Posso
I like	Gosto
I go	Vou
I have / I must	Tenho

I want to go to my house
Eu quero ir a minha casa
I can go with you to the bus station
Eu posso ir contigo para a estação de ônibus
I need to walk outside the muesum
Eu preciso caminhar fora deste museu
I like to eat oranges
Eu gosto de comer uma laranjas
I am going to teach a class
Eu vou para ensinar uma classe
I have to speak to my teacher
Tenho que falar com meu professor

*In Portuguese similar to Spanish, *I have, tenho* when followed by a verb you must always place a *que* proceeding the *tengo*, or *ter* (infinitive form of *to have*). *I have to speak, tenho que falar*. To learn more please see page #44.

Please master pages #16-#38, prior to attempting the following two pages!!

You want / do you want	Você quer
He wants / does he want	Ele quer
She wants / does she want	Ela quer
We want / do we want	Nós queremos
They want / do they want	Eles/elas querem
You (plural) want	Vocês querem

You need / do you need	Você precisa
He needs / does he need	Ele precisa
She needs / does she need	Ela precisa
We want / do we want	Nós precisamos
They need / do they need	Eles/elas precisam
You (plural) need	Vocês precisam

You can / can you	Você pode
He can / can he	Ele pode
She can / can she	Ela pode
We can / can we	Nós podemos
They can / can they	Eles/elas Podem
You (plural) can	Vocês podem

You like / do you like	Você gosta
He likes / does he like	Ele gosta
She like / does she like	Ela gosta
We like / do we like	Nós gostamos
They like / do they like	Eles/elas gostam
You (plural) like	Vocês gostam

You go / do you go	Você vai
He goes / does he go	Ele vai
She goes / does she go	Ela vai
We go / do we go	Nós vamos
They go / do they go	Eles/elas vão
You (plural) go	Vocês vão

You have / do you have	Você tem
He has / does he have	Ele tem
She has / does she have	Ela tem
We have / do we have	Nós temos
They have / do they have	Eles/elas têm
You (plural) have	Vocês têm

Do you want to go?
Você quer ir?
Does he want to fly?
Ele quer voar?
We want to swim
Queremos nadar
Do they want to run?
Querem correr
Do you need to clean?
Você precisa limpar?
She needs to sing a song
Ela precisa cantar um canção
We need to travel
Precisamos viajar
They don't need to fight
Eles não precisam lutar
You (plural) need to see
Vocês precisam ver
Can you hear me?
Pode me escuctar?
He can dance very well
Pode dançar muito bem
We can go out tonight
Podemos sair esta noite
They can break the wood
Podem quebrar la madera
Do you like to eat here?
Gosta de comer aqui?

He likes to spend time here
Gosta de passar tempo aqui
We like to fix the house
Gostamos de arrumar a casa
They like to cook
Eles gostam de cozinhar
You (plural) like my house
Vocês gostam da minha casa
Do you go to school today?
Você vai à escola hoje
He goes fishing
Ele vai pescar
We are going to relax
Vamos relaxar
They go to watch a film
Eles vão ver um filme
Do you have money?
Você tem dinheiro?
She has to look outside
Ela tem que olhar para fora
We have to sign our names
Temos que assinar os nossos nomes
They have to send the letter
Eles tem que mandar/enviar a carta
You (plural) have to order
Vocês tem que ordem

*Whenever refering to a group in which you have all female individuals, you refer to that group as ELAS. Mixed male and female individuals refer to them as ELES.

BASIC GRAMMATICAL REQUIREMENTS OF THE PORTUGUESE LANGUAGE WHICH YOU WILL ENCOUNTER IN THIS PROGRAM

Feminine and Masculine & Plural and Singular

In the Portuguese language there is plural and singular, as well as masculine and feminine. For example the article "*the*", for Portuguese words ending with an *a*, *e*, and *i*, will usually be deemed as feminine, the article will usually be *A*. For nouns ending with an *O*, it will generally be masculine, and the article will usually be *o*. The article the in plural form will be *Os* for masculine form, and *As* for feminine form. *"The boy"* will be *"o (the) menino (boy)"* "*the girl*" will be *"a menina"*, "*the boys*" will be *"os meninos"* and "*the girls*" will be *"as meninas"*.

Although there are exceptions, words which end with *ma*, *pa*, and *ta* the article will usually be *el*.

The article *"a"* (*um* and *uma)*, its conjugation is determined by feminine and masculine form *"a car"* "*um carro"*, *"a house"* "*uma casa"*. In plural form

The conjugation for *This (Esta, este, estes, & estas)* and *That (esse, essa, esses, essas)*. *This, Este* is masculine, *Este Livro, this book*. Feminine would be *esta, Esta casa, this house*. *Estes Livros, these books / Essas casas, these houses* will be the plural form. *That, esse* is masculine, *esse livro, that book*. Feminine would be *essa; Essa cadeira, that chair*. In plural, *esses livros, these books / essas cadeiras, these chairs*.

Of, contains singular and plural form as well, *do* and *dos*.

Basic Grammatical Requirements of the Portuguese Language

Isso and *Isto* are neuter pronouns, meaning they don't have a gender. They usually refer to an idea or an unknown object that isn't specifically named. For example *That; Isto. Isto é, that is / por isso, because of that. This; Isto. Isto esta bom, this is good / O que é isto?, what is this?*

In regards to *my*, singular and plural form exists as well as feminine and masculine. *Meu* is masculine *minha* is feminine, *meus* is masculine plural and *minha* is fem plural. My chair, *minha cadeira / My chairs, minhas cadeiras,* my money, meu dinheiro / my papers, meus papéis. With regard to *your;* (masc) *teu* and (fem) *tua,* plural *teus* and *tuas*. Example in masc singular; *teu carro, your car / your housa, tua casa*. The plural teus carro and tuas casas.

Temporary and Permanent

The different forms of is, *é* and *está* . When refering to a permanent condition, for example *she is a girl, ela é uma menina,* then you use *é*. For temporary position, *the girl is doing well today, a menina está muito bem hoje,* then you use *est á*.

You are / are you; could mean *você está*, it could also mean *você é*. Você está is a temporary postion for example *"How are you today" "Como você está,"* also *"you are here" "você está aqui"*. Você é is a permanent position.

Another example of permanent position *"are you Mexican?", "você é Mexicano?"* also *"You are a man!", "você é um homem!"*

I am, Estou and *eu sou. Eu sou* refers to a permanent conditon, *"I am Italian", "eu sou Italiano."* Temporary condition *"I am at the mall" "Estou no mall"*.

We are; Somos (permanent) and *estamos* (temporary).
Nós somos Peruanos, we are Peruvian. Nos Estamos no parque, we are at the park.

Are; São (permanent), *Estão* (temporary). *Eles* **são** *Chilenos,* they **are** *Chileans. Eles* **estão** *no carro, they* **are** *in the car.*

Synonyms and Antonyms

There are 3 ways of describing *Time:*
*Vez / Vezes - First time, Primeira vez / three **times**, três **vezes***
*Tempo - during the **time** of the dinousaurs, durante o tempo dos dinossauros*
*Hora - What **time** is it?, Que **hora** são?*

***Que* has 4 definitions:**
*What - O **Que** é isso? **What** is this?*
*Than - Eu estou melhor **que** você, I am better **than** you*
*That - I want to say **that** I am near the house, eu quero dezir **que** estou perto de casa*

*I Must / I have to - Tenho **que**.* The verb *ter, to have,* whether it's in conjugated or infitinite form, if it is followed by another verb, then *que* must always follow. For example
*I have to swim now, tenho **que** nadar agora.*

***Deixar* has 2 definitions**
*To leave - Eu quero **deixar** isto aqui, I want to **leave** this here (deixar* is to *leave* something, but when saying *"to leave"* as in *"going"* it's *"sair"*. For example: *I want to leave now, quero sair agora).*
*To allow - **Deixar** could also mean to **allow**.*

There are 2 ways of describing *So*
*So - então. So I need to know, **então** preciso saber.*
So - tão. Isso é tão distante, this is so far.

Verb Conjugation in First Person

The *I, Eu* before a conjugated verb isn't required. For example *Eu preciso saber a data, I need to know the date,* can be said *preciso saber a data.* Because *Preciso* already means *I need* in conjugated form. Although saying *Eu* isn't incorrect! The same can also be said with *você/tu, ele/ela, nos, eles/elas,* in which they aren't required to be placed prior to the conjugated verb, but if they are then it isn't wrong.

Connecting words

In Portuguese certain words can connect, creating one syllable, for example:
The article *the*, in masculine form **o**, feminine form **a**
*In(em)+the(o)=**no**, in the car,**no** caro*
*em+a=**na**, in the house, **na**casa*
In(em) and this(essa), **em+essa; nessa**; *In this house,* **nessa** *casa*
In this car; **em+esse; nesse** *carro*
*em+este = **neste; neste** carro*
*em+esta = **nesta** casa*
*In(em) his(ele) = **nele**; in his car,* **nele** *carro*
*In(em) her(ela) = **nela**; in her house,* **nela** *carro*
Our house, **Nossa** *casa / Our car,* **Nosso** *carro*

His car, **de+ele** *= carro* **dele** */ her car, carro* **dela**
Their car, carro **deles** */ (fem) their car / carro* **delas**

Of and *this* can connect as well creating one syllable,
de+isso; I need this, eu preciso **disso**
de+esse; from this side, **desse** *lado*
de+esses; these men, **desses** *homes*
de+essas; these women, **dessas** *mulheres*
*de+isso = **disto***
*de+aqui = **daqui***
*de+onde = **donde***
*de+outro = **doutro***

OTHER USEFUL TOOLS FOR THE PORTUGUESE LANGUAGE

Reading and Pronunciation

Ç - is pronounced like *s*, whenever it precedes *a,o,u*. *Criança* will be pronounced as *criansa*

D - whenever preceding an *i* or an *e* it pronounced as *dj*. *Tarde* will be pronounced as *tardje*, *dia* will be pronounced as *gia*

H - silent except when followed by an *n*

L - whenever it proceeds an *a* or *i* its pronounced as *ee-oo*; *Brasil* will be pronounced as *Bra-zee-oo*

M - whenever its the last letter of a word then its pronounced as a soft *m*. One trick for pronunciation is saying it without closing your lips.

R - is pronounced as an *h* if its the first letter of the word; *Roberto* will be *Hoberto*. Whenever r is the last letter of a word then its pronounced very softly.

S - pronounced like a *z* whenever it's in between vowels, or when its at the end of the word. *Português* will be pronounced as *Portuguêz*.

T - pronounced as *tchi* whenever preceding an *e* or an *i*, *contigo* will be pronounced as *contchigo*

U - is pronounced like *oo*

W - pronounced like a *v*, *William* will be pronounced as *Villiam*

X - whenever preceding a vowel it will usuually be pronounced as *sh*, *deixar* pronounced as *deishar*. Whenever preceding a consonant it will usually be pronounced as *s*, *exterior* will be pronounced as *esterior*. When in between vowels usually pronounced as *ks*, *fixo* will be *fikso*. Words which begin in *ex* or *hex*, and followed by a vowel, the *x* is pronounced like a *z*, *hexágono* will be *hezágono*.

But in Portuguese x, is one of those letter that there are no set rules for it's pronunciation!

Z - whenever its at the end of a word it's pronounced as a *ss*. *Alvarez* will be pronounced as *Alvaress*.

Diphthongs

ai - is pronounced like the ie in pie
ão - is pronounced like the ow in clown
au - is pronounced like the ow in now
ei - is pronounced like the ay in pay
eu - is pronounced as ay-oo like the ay in hay + the oo in boot
ho - is pronounced like a soft o
ia - is pronounced ee-ah like the ee in feet + the a in father
ie - is pronounced like the e in yes
io - is pronounced ee-oh
iu - is pronounced ee-oo like the ee in meet + the oo in loot
oi - is pronounced "closed" like the oy in toy
ou - is pronounced like the ow in glow
õ - is pronounced nasalized
ua - is pronounced like the oo-ah in watch minus the w sound
ue - is pronounced oo-eh like the oo in loot and the ay in day
ui - is pronounced like oo-ee the oo in loot and the ee in meet
uo - is pronounced like the uo in quota

Diagraphs

lh- is pronounced like lli in alligator
nh - is pronounced like ni in minion; or like mañana in Spanish
rr- pronounced like h, terra will be pronounced teh-ha

Accents

Á - is pronounced like the *y* in *fly*, when at the end of the word pronounced like *a* in *another*
À - is pronounced like the *a* in *another*
Â - is pronounced like a long *a*
Ó - is pronounced like *oy*
É - is pronounced like the *a* in *many*
Ê - pronounced like a long *e*
Ì - is pronounced like the *e* in *embrace*
Ó - is pronounced *oy*, when last letter of word like *u* in *jump*
Ô - is pronounced like a long *o*
Ú and **Û** - pronounced like the *oo* in *loot*

Days of the Week

Sunday	Domingo
Monday	Segunda-feira
Tuesday	Terça-feira
Wednesday	Quarta-feira
Thursday	Quinta-feira
Friday	Sexta-feira
Saturday	Sábado

Seasons

Spring	Primavera
Summer	Verão
Autumn	Outono
Winter	Inverno

Cardinal Directions

North	Norte
South	Sul
East	Leste
West	Oeste

Colors

Black	Preto
White	Branco
Gray	Cinza
Red	Vermelho
Blue	Azul
Yellow	Amarelo
Green	Verde
Orange	Laranja
Purple	Roxo
Brown	Marrom

Numbers

One	Um
Two	Dois
Three	Três
Four	Quatro
Five	Cinco
Six	Sies
Seven	Sete
Eight	Oito
Nine	Nove
Ten	Dez

CONGRATULATIONS, NOW YOU ARE ON YOUR OWN!

If you merely absorb the required 350 words, in this book, you will then have acquired the most comprehensive ultimate foundational basis that was ever created to become conversational in the Portuguese language!! After memorizing these 350 words, then, this "conversational foundational basis" that you have just gained will trigger your ability to make improvements in conversational fluency at the rate of the speed of light! However, in order to engage in fluent communication you need a special type of basics, and this book will provide you with just that, guaranteed.

Unlike the current foreign language learning systems presently used in schools and universities, along with books and programs that are available on the market today, that all focus on *EVERYTHING* but being conversational, by contrast, THIS method's sole focus is on becoming conversational in the Portuguese language as well as any other language. Once you have successfully mastered the required words in this book, there are two techniques that, if combined with these essential words, can further enhance your skills and will result in you improving your fluency tenfold. HO*WEVER* THO*SE* T*WO TECHNIQUES* WILL O*NLY* S*UCCEED* IF you have completely and successfully absorbed the 350 words.

The first step is to attend a Portuguese language class that will enable you to sharpen your grammar. You will gain additional vocabulary, learn past and present tenses and if you apply these skills which you learn in the class, together with the 350 words that you have previously memorized, you will be improving your conversational skills ten fold. You will notice that "conversational wise" you will succeed at a much higher rate than any of your other classmates. A simple second technique is to choose Portuguese subtitles, while watching a movie. If you have successfully mastered and grasped these 350 words, then the combination of the two, those words along with the subtitles, will aid you considerably in putting all the grammar into prospective, and again conversational wise you will improve ten fold.

Once you have established a basis of fluent conversation in Portuguese, resulting from those words which you just attained, then every additional word or grammar rule you pick up from there on, can be combined with them (the 350 words) enriching your conversational abilities even more. Basically after the research and studies I conducted with my method over the years, I came to the conclusion that in order to become conversational you first must learn the words AND then learn the grammar.

The Portuguese language is compatible with the mirror translation technique. Likewise with THIS language, you can use this mirror translation technique in order to become conversational, enabling one to communicate even more fluently. Mirror translation is the method of translating a phrase or sentence, word per word from English to Portuguese, by using these imperative words which you have acquired through this program (such as the sentences I used in this book). Latin languages, Middle Eastern languages, Slavic languages along with a few others are also compatible with the mirror translation technique. Though you won't be speaking Shakespearean, you will still be fully understood and conversation-wise, able to get by just fine.

CONCLUSION

CONGRATULATIONS, you have completed all the tools needed to master the Portuguese language and I hope that this has been a valuable learning experience. Now you have sufficient communication skills to be confident enough to embark on a visit to a Portuguese speaking county, impress your friends and boost your resume so GOOD LUCK.

This program is available in other languages as well and it is my fervent hope that my language learning programs will be used for the good and will enable people from all corners of the globe, from all cultures and religions to be able to communicate harmoniously.

Made in the USA
Middletown, DE
04 May 2015